THE **FOOTBALL ICONS** SERIES

THE GREATEST
GOALKEEPERS

SPENCER **MILLER** HARRISON **FLORIO**

First Published in 2022 by Paw Kingdom Limited.

978-1-915450-11-1

All rights reserved. This book is not to be reproduced, transmitted or stored in any information retrieval system in any form or by any means without the prior consent of Paw Kingdom Limited.

Disclaimer Notice: All names, characters, trademarks and trade names within this book are the property of the respective owners. This is a book published by Paw Kingdom Limited, and has not been licensed, approved, sponsored or endorsed by any person or entity.

Please note that training exercises provided in this book are to be completed at your own risk. Any exercise program may result in injury. By voluntarily undertaking any exercise displayed within this book, you assume the risk of any resulting injury. The contents of this book is to be used for entertainment purposes only.

This book is accurate as of August 2022, all information and facts contained have been checked and verified by Paw Kingdom Limited, and are subject to change. This title focuses on men's football exclusively.

www.PawKingdom.co.uk
info@PawKingdom.co.uk

CONTENTS

| 1 | Greatest of Today | 8 |
| 2 | Legendary Keepers | 42 |

INTRODUCTION

It's no secret that goalkeepers are a different breed! Whilst most kids grow up dreaming of scoring the winning goal for their team, goalkeepers think differently... For most the idea of jumping, high into the air, to try and get your body in the way of the ball that has been smashed goalbound by a striker is a terrifying thought. But not for keepers. For keepers, there is nothing better, nothing more exciting than making a fingertip save, stopping the opposition from scoring and keeping a clean sheet.

Goalkeeping has changed... A LOT! Early goalkeepers, when the rule-makers were still figuring the laws of football, couldn't even hold the ball without opposition players attacking them! So the first keepers had to be strong and robust to even stand a chance. As football evolved, keepers were picked less for their strength and more for their shot-stopping ability. The likes of Yashin and Banks were some of the best keepers of their day, and used their cat-like reactions to stop shots from all angles.

But like everything in life, football continues to evolve and change, and the position of goalkeeper has changed more than most. With the turn of the century, goalkeepers like Manuel Neuer rewrote the book on how to be a goalkeeper, with his sweeping ability and ability to read the game from the back. The Brazilian duo of Ederson and

Allison would follow in his footsteps, as great sweepers and they would add yet another feature to the position of goalkeeper... unbelievable ability with the ball at their feet. Perhaps today's two finest number ones, Ederson and Allison can play football just as well as many of their outfield teammates, making them incredibly valuable when their teams look to build out from the back.

These days, as you will see throughout the book, there are so many different styles of goalkeepers. Every keeper has their own strengths and weaknesses, and every team wants a keeper to fit with their overall play style. So, if you are a keeper at home reading this, and you are a wonderful shot-stopper, but you're not as comfortable at sweeping, or playing with the ball at your feet... DON'T PANIC! Just look at Liverpool and Manchester United, two of the Premier League's biggest teams. Liverpool's Allison loves to play with the ball at his feet, whilst De Gea is less comfortable with the ball at his feet but is a world-class shot-stopper. Work hard, keep training at both your strengths and weaknesses, and you can be very valuable between the sticks for your team.

You might be thinking, why is it important to learn about the greatest goalkeepers? Well, what every goalkeeper (and footballer for that matter) has in common, is that they will all tell you that they learned their skills by studying and analysing the best players before them. By learning about the best to have ever played the game before you, you can grow as a player yourself, and add different elements to your game. So, not only is it super fun and very interesting to look at some of the best keepers ever, it can be incredibly useful for you as a goalkeeper to take your game to the next level!

So turn over the page, learn all about the greatest goalkeepers, and get out there and make sure to always enjoy playing the beautiful game!

THANK YOU!

Thanks for reading! if you enjoy please consider leaving us a review as it means a lot!

Spencer Miller & Harry Florio

DAVID
DE GEA
SPAIN

POSITION(s):
GOALKEEPER

DATE OF BIRTH:
07/11/1990

WEIGHT:
76kg

HEIGHT:
6'4

FOOT:

TEAM HISTORY
2009-2011 - Atletico Madrid
2011-Present - Man United

TEAM HONOURS
Premier League x1
FA Cup x1
League Cup x1
Europa League x2
Super Cup x1

INDIVIDUAL HONOURS
Premier League Golden Glove x1

Manchester United legend David De Gea began his playing career with Atletico Madrid, rising through the academy system at the club before making his senior debut in 2009, aged 18, later becoming the club's first choice goalkeeper that very season. In his first season, he helped the team win the Europa League and followed that up by winning the Super Cup in his second (and final) season in Madrid.

De Gea joined current club Manchester United in 2011 for £18.9 million, a British record for a goalkeeper at the time. Since joining the club, De Gea has made nearly 500 appearances for United as of the end of the 2021/22 Premier League season and has amassed a trophy collection consisting of a Premier League title, an FA Cup, a League Cup, three Community Shields and his second Europa League. De Gea's unrivalled reaction time and shot-stopping ability meant he was elected as United's Sir Matt Busby Player of the Year, not once, not twice, but in three consecutive seasons! He was the first player in the award's history to win on three successive occasions, not bad for a keeper!

De Gea has made a name for himself in the international scene too. He was the captain for the Spain under-21 national team that won the European Championship in 2011 and 2013 and made his debut for the senior team in 2014. De Gea was selected for the 2014 World Cup before being named as Spain's starting goalkeeper for the 2016 European Championship and the 2018 FIFA World Cup.

International Caps	League Games	European Games
45	469	84

*Correct as of AUG 2022

THIBAUT COURTOIS
BELGIUM

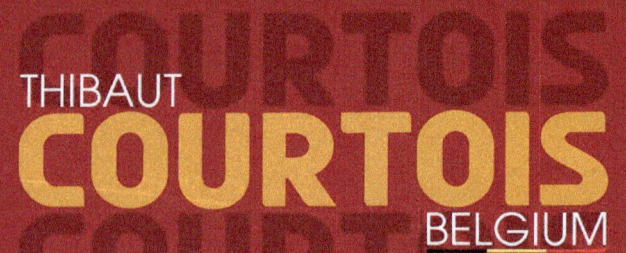

POSITION(s): GOALKEEPER

DATE OF BIRTH: 11/05/1992

WEIGHT: 96kg

HEIGHT: 6'6

FOOT:

TEAM HISTORY
2009-2011 - Genk
2011-2018 - Chelsea
2011-2014 - Atletico Madrid (loan)
2018-Present - Real Madrid

INDIVIDUAL HONOURS
Belgian Professional Goalkeeper of the Year x1
La Liga Goalkeeper of the Season x1
Belgian Sportsman of the Year x1
Premier League Golden Glove x1
World Cup Golden Glove x1
The Best FIFA Goalkeeper x1
IFFHS World's Best Goalkeeper x1

TEAM HONOURS
Belgian Pro League x1
La Liga x3
Copa del Rey x1
Europa League x1
Super Cup x2
Premier League x2
FA Cup x1
League Cup x1
Club World Cup x1
Champions League x1

La Liga's most expensive goalkeeper, Thibaut Courtois joined Real Madrid in 2018 for a record £35million! Since then he has won two La Ligas and a Champions League with Los Blancos, playing a pivotal role in their title wins, even winning man of the match in their 2022 Champions League Final win over Liverpool. This isn't the only success Courtois has experienced in his career however, as he played a key role in Genk's Belgian Pro League victory in 2011 after the youth product became their first team goalkeeper aged just 18 years old. That summer he joined Chelsea for a reported £8 million and was immediately loaned to Atlético Madrid.

In three seasons there, he won the Europa League in 2012, the Copa del Rey in 2013, and the La Liga title in 2014. He also won the Zamora Trophy as La Liga's best goalkeeper in both 2013 and 2014. Courtois returned to Chelsea in 2014, and in his first season, he helped them win the League Cup and the Premier League title. Two years later, he won the Premier League Golden Glove as Chelsea again won the league, before winning the FA Cup in his final season at Stamford Bridge in 2018.

Internationally, Courtois made his senior international debut in 2011, becoming the youngest goalkeeper to represent Belgium. He has since represented his nation at major tournaments such as the 2014 & 2018 World Cups, and the 2016 & 2020 Euro Championships, even picking up the Golden Glove award as the best goalkeeper of the 2018 World Cup.

International Caps	League Games	European Games
94	413	83

*Correct as of AUG 2022

BECKER
ALISSON
BRAZIL

POSITION(s):
GOALKEEPER

DATE OF BIRTH:
02/10/1992

WEIGHT:
91kg

HEIGHT:
6'3

FOOT:

TEAM HISTORY
2013-2016 - Internacional
2016-2018 - Roma
2018-Present - Liverpool

TEAM HONOURS
Premier League x1
Champions League x1
Club World Cup x1
Copa America x1
FA Cup x1
League Cup x1

INDIVIDUAL HONOURS
Serie A Goalkeeper of the Year x1
UEFA Champions League Goalkeeper of the Season x1
The Best FIFA Men's Goalkeeper x1
Premier League Golden Glove x2
Globe Soccer Awards Best Goalkeeper of the Year x2
Copa América Golden Glove x1
IFFHS World's Best Goalkeeper x1
Yashin Trophy x1

One of the best goalkeepers in world football, Brazilian superstar Alisson Becker started his career after progressing through Internacional's academy, making his senior debut in 2013. During his four years with Internacional's senior side, Alisson won the Campeonato Gaucho title in each season. He signed for Roma in 2016 but was used as a backup to first-team goalkeeper Wojciech Szczesny for the entirety of his first season at the club. However, he became first choice in his second season and excelled, winning the Serie A Goalkeeper of the Year award for the 2017/18 season.

His performances led to Alisson joining Liverpool in 2018 for a then-world record fee of approximately £66.8 million and has since experienced a multitude of team and personal accolades. After winning the Champions League in his debut season with the club, as well as winning the Premier League Golden Glove, he was named the Best FIFA Goalkeeper at the end of the year and won the inaugural Yashin Trophy for best performing goalkeeper. Since then he has experienced success by winning the Premier League, Club World Cup, FA Cup, and the League Cup.

The shot-stopper has also provided us with some amazing moments at the other end of the pitch too, such as his last-minute header in Liverpool's 2-1 win against West Brom in 2021! Internationally, Alisson is the preferred goalkeeper for Brazil over fellow world-class goalkeeper, Ederson, and has represented his nation as first-choice keeper in the 2018 World Cup and 2019 Copa America, helping Brazil win the latter competition.

International Caps	League Games	European Games
55	217	61

*Correct as of AUG 2022

… EDOUARD
MENDY
SENEGAL

POSITION(s):
GOALKEEPER

DATE OF BIRTH:
01/03/1992

WEIGHT:
86kg

HEIGHT:
6'4

FOOT:

TEAM HISTORY
2016-2019 - Reims
2019-2020 - Rennes
2020-Present - Chelsea

TEAM HONOURS
Ligue 2 x1
Champions League x1
Super Cup x1

INDIVIDUAL HONOURS
Ghana Football Awards Best African International x1
Champions League Goalkeeper of the Season x1
The Best FIFA Goalkeeper x1

Senegalese goalkeeper Edouard Mendy's journey as a professional goalkeeper is a heartfelt one. After being released by AS Cherbourg in the third-tier of French football, Mendy looked for jobs away from football aged 22, before eventually signing for Marseilles a year later as their fourth-choice goalkeeper...

After one year and zero appearances, Mendy searched for first-team football and eventually joined Ligue 2 side Reims, where he truly showed his abilities, helping them secure the Ligue 2 title in his second season. He was again influential in his third season at the club as helped Reims to an 8th place finish in his first season as a Ligue 1 goalkeeper.

From Reims, he would join Rennes in 2019 for a season and be instrumental in their Champions League qualification campaign as they finished third in the 2019/2020 Ligue 1 season. This would earn him a £22million move to Premier League giants Chelsea, where he would win the Champions League in his debut season and break the Champions League record for most clean sheets in one season. His major turnaround in his career led him to become the 2021 FIFA Best Goalkeeper and carry his national team to their first Africa Cup of Nations in 2022, as he saved a penalty in their penalty shootout win over Egypt and winning the competition's Goalkeeper of the Tournament award.

His meteoric rise between the sticks is certainly one of football's greatest ever fairytale stories.

International Caps	League Games	European Games
25	205	25

*Correct as of AUG 2022

MOST CLEAN SHEETS IN THE 21ST CENTURY

#	Name	Clean Sheets
1	Iker Casillas	439
2	Gianluigi Buffon	420
3	Petr Cech	391
4	Pepe Reina	343
5	Manuel Neuer	327
6	Igor Akinfeev	316
7	Andriy Pyatov	269
8	Edwin van Der Sar	266
9	Victor Valdes	260

Accurate as of August 2022

"Most kids dream of scoring the perfect goal. I've always dreamed of **stopping** it"

IKER CASILLAS

MARC-ANDRE
TER STEGEN
GERMANY

POSITION(s): GOALKEEPER
DATE OF BIRTH: 30/04/1992
WEIGHT: 85kg
HEIGHT: 6'2
FOOT:

TEAM HISTORY
2010-2014 - Monchengladbach
2014-Present - Barcelona

INDIVIDUAL HONOURS
kicker Bundesliga Goalkeeper of the Season x1
UEFA Save of the Season x1

TEAM HONOURS
La Liga x4
Copa del Rey x5
Champions League x1
Super Cup x1
Club World Cup x1

18

German and Barcelona goalkeeper Marc-Andre Ter Stegen began his professional career at Borussia Monchengladbach after rising through the ranks. He became Gladbach's first-choice goalkeeper aged 18 in 2011 and went on to make 108 league appearances for the German side, becoming one of the league's best goalkeepers during his tenure. In 2014, aged just 22, he joined Barcelona for €12 million. In his first season at Barcelona, Ter Stegen won the treble, being the first-choice goalkeeper for the club's Copa del Rey and Champions League matches, but failing to make an appearance in the league. During the club's successful Champions League campaign, Ter Stegen won the 'Best Save' award for his spectacular goal-line save against Bayern Munich in the second leg of the Champions League semi-final.

Since then, Ter Stegen became Barcelona's first-choice keeper in all competitions and went on to win three more La Liga titles, four more Copa del Rey titles, a Super Cup, and a Club World Cup. The ball-playing keeper has also represented Germany consistently since his senior international debut in 2012, despite the presence of German legend Manuel Neuer. He was part of the German squads that reached the semi-finals of UEFA Euro 2016 and won the 2017 FIFA Confederations Cup, and was also a member of the German side that took part in the 2018 World Cup, earning himself a winners medal despite being reserve to goalkeeping legend Manuel Neuer.

International Caps	League Games	European Games
28	326	86

*Correct as of AUG 2022

MORAES
EDERSON
BRAZIL

POSITION(s):
GOALKEEPER

DATE OF BIRTH:
17/08/1993

WEIGHT:
86kg

HEIGHT:
6'2

FOOT:

TEAM HISTORY
2011-2012 - Ribeirao
2012-2015 - Rio Ave
2015-2017 - Benfica
2017-Present - Man City

INDIVIDUAL HONOURS
LPFP Primeira Liga Goalkeeper of the Year x1
Premier League Golden Glove x3

TEAM HONOURS
Primeira Liga x2
Taça de Portugal x1
Taça da Liga x1
Premier League x4
FA Cup x1
League Cup x4
Copa America x1

Like many of the goalkeepers in this book, Ederson had at one point broken the world record for most expensive goalkeeper of all time when he sealed a £35million move from Benfica to Manchester City. However, it all started for Ederson at Brazilian side Sao Paulo in 2008 and, after just one season, he quickly moved into Europe after joining Portuguese side Benfica. He would leave the club for fellow Portuguese clubs Ribeirao and Rio Ave to get more first-team football, before rejoining Benfica four years later in 2015. In two years, Ederson would win two successful Primeira Liga titles as well as one Taca de Portuga and one Taca da Liga. It was then he attracted interest from Premier League club Manchester City, who joined the club for a record £35million.

In his debut season, the free passing Brazilian won the Premier League before doing one better the following year, winning the domestic treble! Whilst at the club, Ederson has won four Premier League titles, one FA Cup and four League Cups, as well as helping the club reach their first ever Champions League Final in 2021. He has also experienced international success with the Brazil national team, such as winning the 2019 Copa America, where he and another world-class goalkeeper Alisson Becker battle for the No.1 spot.

Ederson is known for being as good with his feet as he is with his hands, many even saying he could play in midfield - he is THAT good with the ball at his feet. As teams begin to build their attacks from the back, Ederson is the ultimate modern keeper, and his trophy cabinet proves how effective he has been!

International Caps	League Games	European Games
18	289	60

*Correct as of AUG 2022

JORDAN PICKFORD
ENGLAND

POSITION(s): GOALKEEPER

DATE OF BIRTH: 07/03/1994

WEIGHT: 77kg

HEIGHT: 6'1

FOOT:

TEAM HISTORY
2011-2017 - Sunderland
2017-Present - Everton

TEAM HONOURS
Toulon Tournament x1

INDIVIDUAL HONOURS
Everton Player of the Season x1
Everton Players' Player of the Season x1
Everton Young Player of the Season x1
England Under-21 Player of the Year x1
Premier League Save of the Season x1

22

Sunderland youth graduate Jordan Pickford first made a name for himself during the 2016/17 Premier League season when he was Sunderland's No.1 following an injury to senior goalkeeper Vito Mannone. The following summer he would become Britain's most expensive goalkeeper after a £30 million move to Everton.

200 appearances later, Pickford has been an everpresent name on Everton's teamsheet for the last five years and in turn, earning him the number one spot for the England National Team. Pickford would be Gareth Southgate's first choice between the sticks during the 2018 World Cup, helping England reach their first semi-final since 1990. He would be crucial in England's Round of 16 victory over Colombia, saving a penalty as England beat Colombia on penalties after a 1-1 draw, England's first ever World Cup penalty shoot-out victory. In the quarter-final, Pickford kept a clean sheet and won the man of the match award as England knocked out Sweden with a 2-0 win.

Pickford also became the first goalkeeper in history to keep clean sheets in the first five games of a European Championship during the 2020 Euros, also setting an all-time England record for most consecutive scoreless minutes posted by a goalkeeper. England would get to the Final of the 2020 Euros and Pickford would save 2 Italy penalties during a penalty shoot-out, however, England would go on to lose to Italy 3-2 on penalties.

*International Caps	League Games	European Games
45	327	6

*Correct as of AUG 2022

MOST CLEAN SHEETS AT THE WORLD CUP

#	Name	Clean Sheets
1	Fabien Barthez	10
2	Peter Shilton	10
3	Claudio Taffarel	8
4	Sepp Maier	8
5	Emerson Leao	8
6	Iker Casillas	7
7	Manuel Neuer	7
8	Gilmar	7
9	Gianluigi Buffon	6

Accurate as of August 2022

24

> You score goals as a kid. Then grow up stupid and become a goalkeeper!
>
> **GIANLUIGI BUFFON**

HUGO
LLORIS
FRANCE

POSITION(s):
GOALKEEPER

DATE OF BIRTH:
26/12/1986

WEIGHT:
82kg

HEIGHT:
6'2

FOOT:

TEAM HISTORY
2005-2008 - Nice
2008-2012 - Lyon
2012-Present - Spurs

TEAM HONOURS
Coupe de France x1
FIFA World Cup 1x
UEFA Nations League x1

INDIVIDUAL HONOURS
Ligue 1 Goalkeeper of the Year x3

26

Tottenham Hotspur legend Hugo Lloris has been one of the most consistent performers in the Premier League since his move to North London in 2012. Prior to his Spurs move, Lloris enjoyed a successful spell at Lyon after he signed for the 2007/08 Ligue 1 champions the summer after. Despite not winning a Ligue 1 title himself, Lloris would go on to win three Ligue 1 Goalkeeper of the Year awards and be named in the Ligue 1 Team of the Year three times during his four-year spell.

After his €15 million move to Spurs, he became the club's preferred goalkeeper and would keep this role for the next 10 years, even being named as the club's first team captain in 2015. Lloris captained Spurs to their first ever Champions League Final in 2019, narrowly losing out to fellow English side Liverpool as they lost 2-0 on the night.

Lloris also captains his national side as well as his club side after he was named the permanent first-team captain of France in 2012. Internationally he would lead France to consecutive finals as the French were defeated in extra-time during the 2016 European Championship, but made up for it by lifting the 2018 World Cup after a 4-2 victory over Croatia. Lloris had a nervy moment in the final, where he gifted the Croatians a goal with some slightly too casual footwork, but he more than made up for it with his performances throughout the tournament for Les Bleus.

International Caps	League Games	European Games
139	574	104

*Correct as of AUG 2022

AARON
RAMSDALE
ENGLAND

POSITION(s):
GOALKEEPER

DATE OF BIRTH:
14/05/1998

WEIGHT:
77kg

HEIGHT:
6'2

FOOT:

TEAM HISTORY
2016-2017 - Sheffield United
2017-2020 - Bournemouth
2020-2021 - Sheffield United
2021-Present - Arsenal

TEAM HONOURS
European Under-19 Championship x1
Toulon Tournament x1

INDIVIDUAL HONOURS
Bournemouth Supporters' Player of the Year x1
Sheffield United Player of the Year x1
Sheffield United Young Player of the Year x1

28

England and Arsenal goalkeeper Aaron Ramsdale is a growing name amongst English football ever since he broke through into the Bournemouth first team in 2019. Aged just 21, Ramsdale started the season as Bournemouth's preferred choice as a number one and went on to start 37 of the 38 Premier League games that season, only missing one match due to injury. His fine form that season earnt him the club's Player of the Season award before his former club Sheffield United splashed £18.5million to return him to the club.

Again, Ramsdale was ever-present for Sheffield United during their Premier League season, starting in all 38 Premier League games. However, just like his previous season at Bournemouth, Ramsdale could not survive relegation as Sheffield United finished 20th during the 2020/21 Premier League season. Nevertheless, another fine personal season for Ramsdale saw him pick up the club's Player of the Year and Young Player of the Year awards as well as attracting interest from many Premier League clubs.

In 2021, after only a season at Sheffield United, Ramsdale signed for Arsenal in a club-record transfer worth up to £30 million, becoming their most expensive goalkeeper of all time. His first season with the Gunners was another strong season for Ramsdale, putting in some brilliant performances and winning the club's Player of the Month award on two occasions, whilst performing a save that some pundits called the greatest in Premier League history.

*International Caps	League Games	European Games
3	152	0

*Correct as of AUG 2022

GIANLUIGI DONNARUMMA
ITALY

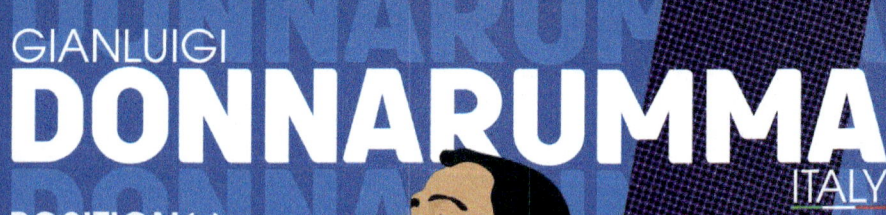

POSITION(s):
GOALKEEPER

DATE OF BIRTH:
25/02/1999

WEIGHT:
90kg

HEIGHT:
6'5

FOOT:

TEAM HISTORY
2015-2021 - AC Milan
2021-Present - PSG

TEAM HONOURS
Euro Championships x1
Ligue 1 x1

INDIVIDUAL HONOURS
Goal.com NxGn x1
Italian Golden Boy Award x1
AIC Serie A Goalkeeper of the Year x1
Serie A Best Goalkeeper x1
IFFHS World's Best Goalkeeper x1
Euro Championships Player of the Tournament x1
Globe Soccer Awards Best Goalkeeper of the Year x1
Yashin Trophy x1

30

PSG and Italy goalkeeper Gianluigi Donnarumma has been one of the more consistent performing goalkeepers since he made his debut 7 years ago. After coming through their youth system, Donnarumma began his career with AC Milan in 2015 and became the second-youngest goalkeeper ever to debut in Serie A, aged just 16 years old. After his debut, he immediately broke into the starting line-up and earned a reputation as arguably the most promising young goalkeeper in the world at the time. Even now, after 7 years of being a first-choice goalkeeper, it's hard to believe Donnarumma is still only 23 years old!

In 2021, Donnarumma helped Milan secure a second-place finish in the 2020–21 Serie A and qualification for the 2021–22 UEFA Champions League after an eight-year absence. He was also named Serie A's Best Goalkeeper of the Year, IFFHS World's Best Goalkeeper and also won the Yashin Trophy. After six years with Milan, Donnarumma moved to Ligue 1 side PSG in June 2021 on a free transfer, winning the league title in his first season in Paris.

Internationally, Donnarumma became the youngest goalkeeper ever to appear for Italy in 2016, aged 17 years old, and became Italy's first-choice goalkeeper during a major tournament when he was called up for the Euro 2020 tournament. He was instrumental as Italy won the tournament, with Donnarumma winning the Player of the Tournament award after his penalty heroics defeated England in the final.

International Caps	League Games	European Games
47	232	27

*Correct as of AUG 2022

MOST CLEAN SHEETS IN THE CHAMPIONS LEAGUE

1	Iker Casillas	1398
2	Manuel Neuer	1285
3	Gianluigi Buffon	1226
4	Edwin van der Sar	1210
5	Petr Cech	1187
6	Victor Valdes	1170
7	Dida	1157
8	**Oliver Kahn**	1125
9	Vitor Baia	1105

Accurate as of August 2022

> **Goalkeepers need an element of insanity!**
> **OLIVER KAHN**

KEYLOR NAVAS
COSTA RICA

POSITION(s):
GOALKEEPER

DATE OF BIRTH:
15/12/1986

WEIGHT:
80kg

HEIGHT:
6'1

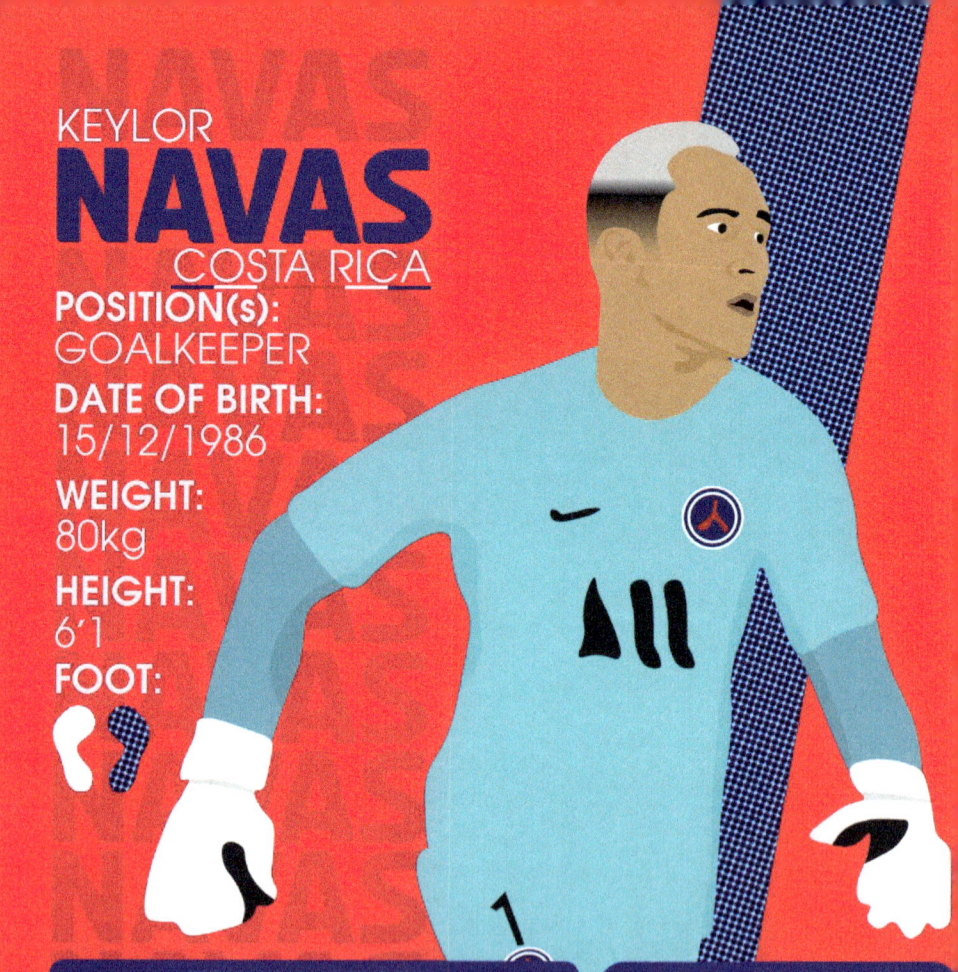

FOOT:

TEAM HISTORY
2012-2014 - Levante
2014-2019 - Real Madrid
2019-Present - PSG

TEAM HONOURS
La Liga x1
Ligue 1 x2
Coupe de France x2
Champions League x3
Super Cup x3
Club World Cup x4

INDIVIDUAL HONOURS
La Liga Best Goalkeeper x1
Ligue 1 Goalkeeper of the Year x1
Champions League Goalkeeper of the Season x1
CONCACAF Gold Cup Best Goalkeeper x1

The Costa Rican brick wall started his career in humble beginnings as he played for Costa Rican side Saprissa, winning six Liga FPD titles and the CONCACAF Champions League, before getting his European move to Spain. After spells with Albacete and Levante (where he won the LFP Award for Best Goalkeeper), Navas joined La Liga giants Real Madrid for €10 million in 2014.

There he would establish himself as one of the world's greatest keepers, playing between the sticks in Real Madrid's three consecutive Champions League triumphs between 2016 and 2018. He would also lift a Supercopa de Espana, three Super Cups, four Club World Cups and the 2016/17 edition of La Liga. In his final season at the club, Navas became the first ever non-Spanish goalkeeper to reach 100 La Liga appearances for Real Madrid as he left the club with over 150 appearances in all competitions for the Madrid side.

Navas left Madrid for Paris to play for Ligue 1 giants PSG in 2019, becoming the first Costa Rican to play for the men's team, and won two league titles and two Coupe de France titles in his three seasons at the club so far. Making over 100 caps for his national team, Navas has excelled at both club and international level, winning multiple individual awards. These include UEFA Best Goalkeeper in Europe, three consecutive CONCACAF Men's Goalkeeper of the Year awards and the IFFHS CONCACAF Player of the Decade award!

International Caps	League Games	European Games
107	331	75

*Correct as of AUG 2022

MANUEL NEUER
GERMANY

POSITION(s):
GOALKEEPER

DATE OF BIRTH:
27/03/1986

WEIGHT:
93kg

HEIGHT:
6'4

FOOT:

TEAM HISTORY
2006-2011 - Schalke
2011-Present - Bayern

TEAM HONOURS
Bundesliga x10
DFB-Pokal x6
Champions League x2
Super Cup x2
Club World Cup x2
World Cup x1

INDIVIDUAL HONOURS
Germany National Player of the Year x2
IFFHS World's Best Goalkeeper x5
IFFHS World's Best Goalkeeper of the Decade x1
Best European Goalkeeper x5
UEFA Champions League Goalkeeper of the Season x1
The Best FIFA Men's Goalkeeper x1
FIFA World Cup Golden Glove x1

36

One of the greatest keepers in the history of the sport, Manuel Neuer was voted the goalkeeper of the decade from 2011-2020 thanks to his unreal shop stopping and his quickness when it comes to sweeping up the ball. In fact, his quickness off the line and his ability to command his area have led to some saying that he 'revolutionised' the position and that he epitomises the modern goalkeeper. This is down to his outfield ability as well as his goalkeeping ability, with the big German having brilliant ball control and a comfortable passer, he has even been known to take penalties early in penalty shootouts.

The German's career started at FC Schalke and earned the right to be the club's first-choice goalkeeper in 2006 aged just 20 years of age. Neuer would win the DFB-Pokal in his final season before signing for Bayern Munich in 2011. Whilst in Bavaria, he has won 28 trophies, including ten Bundesliga titles, two Champions League titles (both as part of trebles), and a further five DFB-Pokals. On an individual level, he has been awarded the UEFA Goalkeeper of the Year and the IFFHS World's Best Goalkeeper five times each.

Neuer was selected as Germany's number one goalkeeper for the 2010 FIFA World Cup in South Africa, conceding only three goals during the tournament. Four years later, Neuer would win the World Cup with Germany as well as the Golden Glove award for being the best goalkeeper in the tournament. Even now, late into his thirties, Neuer remains Germany's number one, and one of the world's top shot stoppers.

International Caps	League Games	European Games
113	491	135

*Correct as of AUG 2022

JAN OBLAK
SLOVENIA

POSITION(s):
GOALKEEPER

DATE OF BIRTH:
07/01/1993

WEIGHT:
87kg

HEIGHT:
6'2

FOOT:

TEAM HISTORY
2010-2014 - Benfica
2012-2013 - Rio Ave (loan)
2014-Present - Atletico

TEAM HONOURS
Primeira Liga x1
Taca de Portugal x1
Taca da Liga x1
La Liga x1
Europa League x1
Super Cup x1

INDIVIDUAL HONOURS
Primeira Liga Best Goalkeeper x1
La Liga Best Goalkeeper x1
Slovenian Footballer of the Year x6
La Liga Player of the Season x1

38

Slovenian superstar Jan Oblak signed for Portuguese club Benfica at the age of 17 and rose to prominence when he achieved the Portuguese domestic treble with Benfica during the 2013/14 season aged just 21. His performances earned him a move to Atletico Madrid for a fee of €16 million in the summer of 2014, becoming La Liga's most expensive goalkeeper at the time. After a slow first season in Madrid, Oblak became an impenetrable force between the sticks in his second season and won the Ricardo Zamora Trophy for best goalkeeper during the 2015/16 season, conceding an all-time record low of 18 goals. This was just the start for Oblak, as he won the award again in the following three seasons, and for a fifth time in 2021.

As of the end of the 2021/22 season, Oblak has made over 350 appearances for Atletico Madrid and is the goalkeeper with the most appearances for the club. He has won four trophies whilst playing in Spain, such as the Europa League, Super Cup, Supercopa de Espana, and the 2020/21 edition of La Liga - where he managed to keep 18 clean sheets in 38 matches, in addition to achieving 80% save rate for the season. Internationally, Oblak made his senior international debut for Slovenia in 2012, and was made first choice goalkeeper after the retirement of fellow Slovenian Samir Handanovic in 2015. Oblak has also been named Slovenian Footballer of the Year on six occasions, clearly one of the very best keepers in the history of the game.

International Caps	League Games	European Games
50	365	79

*Correct as of AUG 2022

MOST CLEAN SHEETS IN THE PREMIER LEAGUE

#	Player	Clean Sheets
1	Petr Cech	202
2	David James	169
3	Mark Schwarzer	151
4	David Seaman	141
5	Nigel Martyn	137
6	Pepe Reina	136
7	**David de Gea**	132
8	Brad Friedel	132
9	Edwin van der Sar	132

Accurate as of August 2022

> I train every day to be the best goalkeeper in the world; that is my aim
> **DAVID DE GEA**

GIANLUIGI BUFFON
ITALY

POSITION(s): GOALKEEPER

DATE OF BIRTH: 28/01/1978

WEIGHT: 92kg

HEIGHT: 6'4

FOOT:

CERTIFIED FOOTBALL LEGEND

TEAM HISTORY
1995-2001 - Parma
2001-2018 - Juventus
2018-2019 - PSG
2019-2021 - Juventus
2021-Present - Parma

TEAM HONOURS
Serie A x10
Serie B x1
Coppa Italia x6
UEFA Cup x1
Ligue 1 x1
World Cup x1

INDIVIDUAL HONOURS
Serie A Goalkeeper of the Year x12
UEFA Club Goalkeeper of the Year x2
UEFA Club Footballer of the Year x1
Best European Goalkeeper x3
IFFHS World's Best Goalkeeper x5
IFFHS Best Goalkeeper of the Decade x1
IFFHS Best Goalkeeper of the 21st Century x1
IFFHS All Time World's Best Goalkeeper x1
Serie A Footballer of the Year x1
The Best FIFA Goalkeeper x1

Where to start with the legend that is Gigi Buffon?

Buffon's professional career began with Parma in 1995, helping them win the Coppa Italia, the UEFA Cup and the Supercoppa Italiana all in 1999. His performances for Parma would earn him a world record transfer to fellow Italians Juventus, with a fee of €52 million. Whilst at Juventus, Buffon won a record nine Serie A titles, four Coppa Italias and five Supercoppa Italiana's. He was the first goalkeeper to win the Serie A Footballer of the Year award, was named Serie A Goalkeeper of the Year a record twelve times and won the inaugural The Best FIFA Goalkeeper award in 2017.

After 17 years at Juventus, Buffon left for PSG in Ligue 1, before returning to Juventus for two more seasons after just one year in Paris. During his second spell in Turin, Buffon managed to break Paolo Maldini's record of 647 appearances in Serie A, as he won a record tenth Serie A title with the club and a record sixth Coppa Italia. He returned to boyhood club Parma in 2021 and is still playing at the age of 44! Just goes to Internationally, Buffon is the most capped player in the history of the Italy national team, with 176 international caps, and holds the record for most appearances for Italy as captain after he inherited the armband in 2010. Buffon was called up for a record five World Cup tournaments and was the starting goalkeeper of the squad that won the 2006 tournament, being awarded the Golden Glove as the competition's best goalkeeper. He also represented Italy at four European Championships during his illustrious career.

International Caps	League Games	European Games
176	737	167

*Correct as of AUG 2022

43

JENS LEHMANN
GERMANY

CERTIFIED FOOTBALL LEGEND

POSITION(s):
GOALKEEPER

DATE OF BIRTH:
11/11/1969

WEIGHT:
87kg

HEIGHT:
6'3

FOOT:

TEAM HISTORY
1987-1998 - Schalke 04
1998-1999 - AC Milan
1999-2003 - Borussia Dortmund
2003-2008 - Arsenal
2008-2010 - VfB Stuttgart

TEAM HONOURS
Bundesliga x1
2. Bundesliga x1
Serie A x1
Premier League x1
FA Cup x1
UEFA Cup x1

INDIVIDUAL HONOURS
UEFA Goalkeeper of the Year x2
UEFA Club Best Goalkeeper x1
kicker Bundesliga Team of the Season x1
FIFA World Cup All-Star Team x1

44

One of the game's most iconic goalkeepers, big Jens Lehmann was truly an all-around, world-class player. His style of play acted as an inspiration to current German icon Manuel Neuer and led Jens to become one of the best goalkeepers in the Bundesliga, Premier League and the Champions League.

Starting at FC Schalke, Lehmann made over 300 appearances for the club as well as scoring two goals! He scored his first league goal against 1860 Munich from the penalty spot, before netting against bitter rivals, Borussia Dortmund, in the last minute to equalise in the Revierderby. Lehmann then moved to Milan for half a season before returning to the Bundesliga with former rivals Borussia Dortmund.

After nearly 200 appearances at Dortmund, and breaking the club's record for most red cards by any Dortmund player, (not a record he would love to remember) Lehmann left Germany for the Premier League. In just his first season at Arsenal, he was part of the Gunner's invincible season, having played every match in their unbeaten title-winning season. This was the start of his successful career in North London, which included breaking records such as the Champions League record for the most consecutive clean sheets, from when he didn't concede a single goal in eight consecutive matches. He also has the highest number of continuous minutes without conceding goals in the Champions League, with the big German not conceding in 853 minutes, and was voted UEFA Club Goalkeeper of the Year twice.

International Caps	League Games	European Games
61	621	116

OLIVER KAHN
GERMANY

POSITION(s): GOALKEEPER
DATE OF BIRTH: 15/06/1969
WEIGHT: 91kg
HEIGHT: 6'2
FOOT:

CERTIFIED FOOTBALL LEGEND

TEAM HISTORY
1987-1994 - Karlsruher SC
1994-2008 - Bayern Munich

TEAM HONOURS
Euro Championships x1
UEFA Cup x1
Champions League x1
DFB-Pokal x6
Bundesliga x8

INDIVIDUAL HONOURS
Best Bundesliga Keeper x7
IFFHS World's Best Goalkeeper x3
Best European Goalkeeper x4
UEFA Club Best Goalkeeper x4
German Footballer of the Year x2

46

He started his career in the Karlsruher SC and made his debut aged just 18 in 1987, before being transferred to Bayern Munich in 1994 after becoming a key player for Karlsruher SC. Khan joined Bayern for a fee of €2.385 million, which was a record fee for a goalkeeper at the time, and remained in Bavaria for the remainder of his career.

Der Titan is one of the most successful German players in recent history, but as well as his team successes with Bayern Munich, Oliver Kahn won a multitude of individual awards. The German stopper won eight Bundesliga titles, six DFB-Pokals, the UEFA Cup in 1996 and the Champions League in 2001, but enjoyed just as much individual success such as winning a record four consecutive UEFA Best European Goalkeeper awards, three IFFHS World's Best Goalkeeper awards and two German Footballer of the Year trophies.

From 1994 to 2006, Kahn was part of the German national team and lifted the 1996 European Championship despite not being used once. It wasn't until 1998 that Kahn became Germany's key man between the sticks. Whilst playing for Germany, Khan was one of the nation's key performers and to this day he is the only goalkeeper in World Cup history to win the Golden Ball for being the best player in a World Cup tournament for his efforts during the 2002 tournament.

International Caps	League Games	European Games
86	557	140

MOST PREMIER LEAGUE CLEAN SHEETS SINCE 2020

#	Player	Clean Sheets
1	Ederson	39
2	Alisson	30
3	Edouard Mendy	30
4	Hugo Lloris	28
5	Emiliano Martinez	26
6	Robert Sanchez	21
7	Nick Pope	20
8	Vicente Guaita	19
9	Lukasz Fabianski	18

Accurate as of August 2022
From the beginning of the 2020/21 Premier League season

> Lots of times I have to leave the goal to block a ball
> **EDERSON**

IKER CASILLAS
SPAIN

POSITION(s):
GOALKEEPER

DATE OF BIRTH:
20/05/1981

WEIGHT:
80kg

HEIGHT:
6'0

FOOT:

CERTIFIED FOOTBALL LEGEND

TEAM HISTORY
1999-2015 - Real Madrid
2015-2020 - Porto

INDIVIDUAL HONOURS
La Liga Best Goalkeeper x2
Primeira Liga Best Goalkeeper x1
Best European Goalkeeper x1
IFFHS World's Best Goalkeeper x5
World Cup Golden Glove x1

TEAM HONOURS
La Liga x5
Copa del Rey x2
Champions League x3
Super Cup x2
Club World Cup x1
Primeira Liga x1
Euro Championships x2
World Cup x1

50

Real Madrid icon Iker Casillas was a superstar ever since he emerged from Madrid's youth team aged just 18, starting in and winning the Champions League Final just four days after his 19th birthday. Casillas would then become the first-choice goalkeeper at Real Madrid, winning two Champions Leagues and La Liga titles in his first three seasons, establishing himself as one of the best goalkeepers in the world.

During his highly successful career in Madrid, Casillas won all major club titles, including five La Liga titles, two Copa del Rey titles, three Champions Leagues, two Super Cups, and the FIFA Club World Cup. After 25 years with Real Madrid, Casillas joined FC Porto in 2015 on a free transfer, where he won the Primeira Liga title in 2018. He also broke the record for most consecutive seasons played in the Champions League whilst at Porto, and amassed the most appearances in the competition's history!

With 167 international caps, Casillas went on to lead Spain to the Euros title in 2008. He also led Spain to their first World Cup win in 2010, where he kept a joint record five clean sheets, winning the Yashin Award for the best goalkeeper of the tournament. Spain became the first nation to retain the European Championship, winning the title again in 2012, where he set the record for most consecutive minutes without conceding a goal in the history of the competition.

International Caps	League Games	European Games
167	630	183

VICTOR VALDES
SPAIN

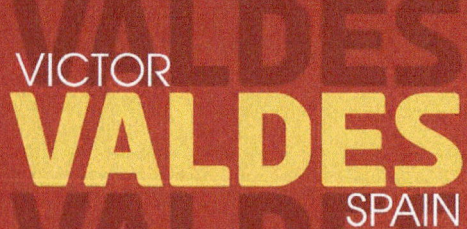

POSITION(s):
GOALKEEPER

DATE OF BIRTH:
14/01/1982

WEIGHT:
78kg

HEIGHT:
6'0

FOOT:

TEAM HISTORY
2002-2014 - Barcelona
2015-2016 - Man United
2016-2017 - Middlesbrough

INDIVIDUAL HONOURS
La Liga Best Goalkeeper x2
Zamora Trophy x5

TEAM HONOURS
La Liga x6
Copa del Rey x2
Champions League x3
Super Cup x2
Club World Cup x2
World Cup x1
Euro Championships x1

Barcelona legend Victor Valdes progressed through the club's youth system at La Masia, eventually earning his first team debut in 2002. It took just one season for Valdes to become Barca's first-choice goalkeeper, playing in 33 league matches during the 2003/04 La Liga season. He would go on to spend most of his professional career with Barcelona, and to this day is regarded as one of the best goalkeepers in the club's history, having appeared in 535 official games for the club. Whilst in Catalonia, Valdes won 21 major titles, notably six La Liga titles and three Champions League titles, and earned many individual accolades such as winning the Zamora Trophy a record five times. He currently holds the club records as the goalkeeper with the most appearances in the league and in official competitive matches.

After 12 years in Barcelona's first team squad, Valdes left the club at the end of his contract in the summer of 2014 after tearing his anterior cruciate ligament (ACL), joining English giants Manchester United midway through the season after his recovery from his injury. He spent two and a half years in England, with his final year being at Middlesborough, and officially retired from football in 2017 after failing to reach the heights he did in Spain whilst in England. Internationally, despite only racking up 20 international caps for Spain (mainly due to Iker Casillas' domination internationally), Valdes was part of the Spain squads which won the 2010 World Cup and Euro 2012.

International Caps	League Games	European Games
20	499	115

PETR CECH

CZECH REPUBLIC

POSITION(s): GOALKEEPER

DATE OF BIRTH: 20/05/1982

WEIGHT: 90kg

HEIGHT: 6'5

FOOT:

TEAM HISTORY
2001-2002 - Sparta Prague
2002-2004 - Rennes
2004-2015 - Chelsea
2015-2019 - Arsenal

TEAM HONOURS
Premier League x4
FA Cup x5
League Cup x3
Champions League x1
Europa League x1

INDIVIDUAL HONOURS
Ligue 1 Best Goalkeeper x1
Premier League Golden Glove x4
Czech Footballer of the Year x9
Czech Republic Golden Ball x12
IFFHS World's Best Goalkeeper x1
Best European Goalkeeper x4
UEFA Club Football Awards Best Goalkeeper x3

Cech began his senior career in his home nation of the Czech Republic and, at the age of 19, he became a first-team regular. In his single campaign with Sparta Prague, Cech registered a league record of not conceding a goal in 903 competitive minutes. This led to his first move abroad when he relocated to France to join Ligue 1 side Rennes for a fee of £3.9 million in 2002. After two years, he was subject of a then club-record transfer for a goalkeeper when he moved to Premier League side Chelsea for a fee of £7 million.

During his eleven-year association with the club, Cech registered 494 senior appearances, making him the club's highest overseas appearance maker, and sixth all-time appearance maker, as well as holding Chelsea's all-time record for clean sheets, with 228. He was vital for the team as the club went on to win four Premier League titles, four FA Cups, three League Cups, one Champions League title, and one Europa League title during his tenure. Cech joined rivals Arsenal in 2010 where he won another FA Cup before retiring in 2019.

Cech holds a number of goalkeeping records including the Premier League record for the fewest appearances required to reach 100 clean sheets, having done so in 180 appearances, the most clean sheets in a season, as well as the record for the most clean sheets in Premier League history. Cech is also the only goalkeeper to have won the Premier League Golden Glove with two separate clubs and has won it a joint record four times.

International Caps	League Games	European Games
124	567	134

55

DIDA
BRAZIL

POSITION(s): GOALKEEPER

DATE OF BIRTH: 07/10/1973

WEIGHT: 85kg

HEIGHT: 6'2

FOOT:

TEAM HISTORY
1994-1998 - Cruzeiro
1999-2000 - Corinthians
2000-2010 - AC Milan
2012-2012 - Portuguesa
2013-2013 - Gremio
2014-2015 - Internacional

INDIVIDUAL HONOURS
Serie A Goalkeeper of the Year x1
FIFPro Goalkeeper of the Year x1
IFFHS Best Brazilian Goalkeeper of the 21st Century

TEAM HONOURS
Copa do Brasil x2
Copa Libertadores x1
Campeonato Brasileiro x1
Club World Cup x2
Serie A x1
Coppa Italia x1
Champions League x2
Super Cup x2
Copa America x1
World Cup x1

Brazilian legend Dida started his senior club career in Brazil with Vitoria, moving to both Cruzeiro and Corinthians in his home nation before he moved to European club AC Milan. Penalty specialist Dida is best remembered for this trophy-ladened 10-year spell at Italian giants Milan, which included two Champions League victories, with Dida fantastically saving three penalties in Milan's 2003 victory over Juventus. He won the competition for a second time in 2007 after a 2-1 victory over Liverpool. He would also win one Scudetto with Milan and be one of just four goalkeepers to make over 300 appearances for the Rossoneri, making him a certified legend at the club. He would return to Brazil to finish his playing career.

Dida also holds a World Cup and Copa America winners medal, as well as winning Olympic Gold at the 1996 Olympics. He has lined up for Brazil on 91 occasions, deeming him one of the best to play for Brazil in his position alongside other legends such as Marcos, Rogerio Ceni, Claudio Taffarel and Gilmar. He has also been recognised for his talents individually, such as winning the inaugural FIFPro Goalkeeper of the Year award and being voted the IFFHS' best Latin American keeper of the 21st century! He is also just one of ten players to win both the Champions League and the Copa Libertadores.

International Caps	League Games	European Games
91	489	86

MOST SAVES IN THE PREMIER LEAGUE

#	Player	Saves
1	Ben Foster	1248
2	David de Gea	1074
3	Lukasz Fabianski	1035
4	Petr Cech	1005
5	Tim Howard	992
6	Joe Hart	941
7	**Hugo Lloris**	918
8	Jussi Jaaskelainen	902
9	Mark Schwarzer	836

Accurate as of August 2022

> You can learn at any age and at any moment in your life
> **HUGO LLORIS**

EDWIN VAN DER SAR

NETHERLANDS

POSITION(s):
GOALKEEPER

DATE OF BIRTH:
29/10/1970

WEIGHT:
83kg

HEIGHT:
6'6

FOOT:

TEAM HISTORY
1990-1999 - Ajax
1999-2001 - Juventus
2001-2005 - Fulham
2005-2011 - Man United

TEAM HONOURS
Eredivisie x4
KNVB Cup x3
Premier League x4
Champions League x2
UEFA Cup x1
Super Cup x1
League Cup x1
Club World Cup x1

INDIVIDUAL HONOURS
Dutch Football Goalkeeper of the Year x4
Best European Goalkeeper x1
Dutch Footballer of the Year x1
Premier League Golden Glove x1
UEFA Club Goalkeeper of the Year x1

Ajax and Manchester United legend Edwin Van der Sar was part of both Ajax and Manchester United's golden generation teams, winning a Champions League with both teams 13 years apart. He started his professional career at the Dutch club, winning the UEFA Cup in his second season, despite not making an appearance in the competition. He went on to win four Eredivisie titles and three KNVB Cups domestically, before winning (and starting in) the 1995 Champions League Final as Ajax defeated AC Milan 1-0, leading to Van der Sar receiving the 1995 Best European Goalkeeper award. He also started the 1996 Champions League Final but settled for a runners-up medal as Ajax lost on penalties to Italian side Juventus. He would leave Ajax after winning four consecutive Dutch Football Goalkeeper of the Year awards.

After brief spells at Juventus and newly promoted Premier League club Fulham, Van der Sar would join Manchester United aged 35, winning four Premier League titles and the 2008 Champions League title, making him one of just eight players at the time to have won the competition with more than one club. He also won a host of individual awards, such as Best European Goalkeeper, UEFA Club Goalkeeper of the Year and the Premier League Golden Glove, as well as breaking multiple records such as the world record of not conceding a league goal for 1,311 minutes and becoming the oldest player to win the Premier League, having done so at the age of 40 years old.

International Caps	League Games	European Games
130	605	139

DAVID SEAMAN
ENGLAND

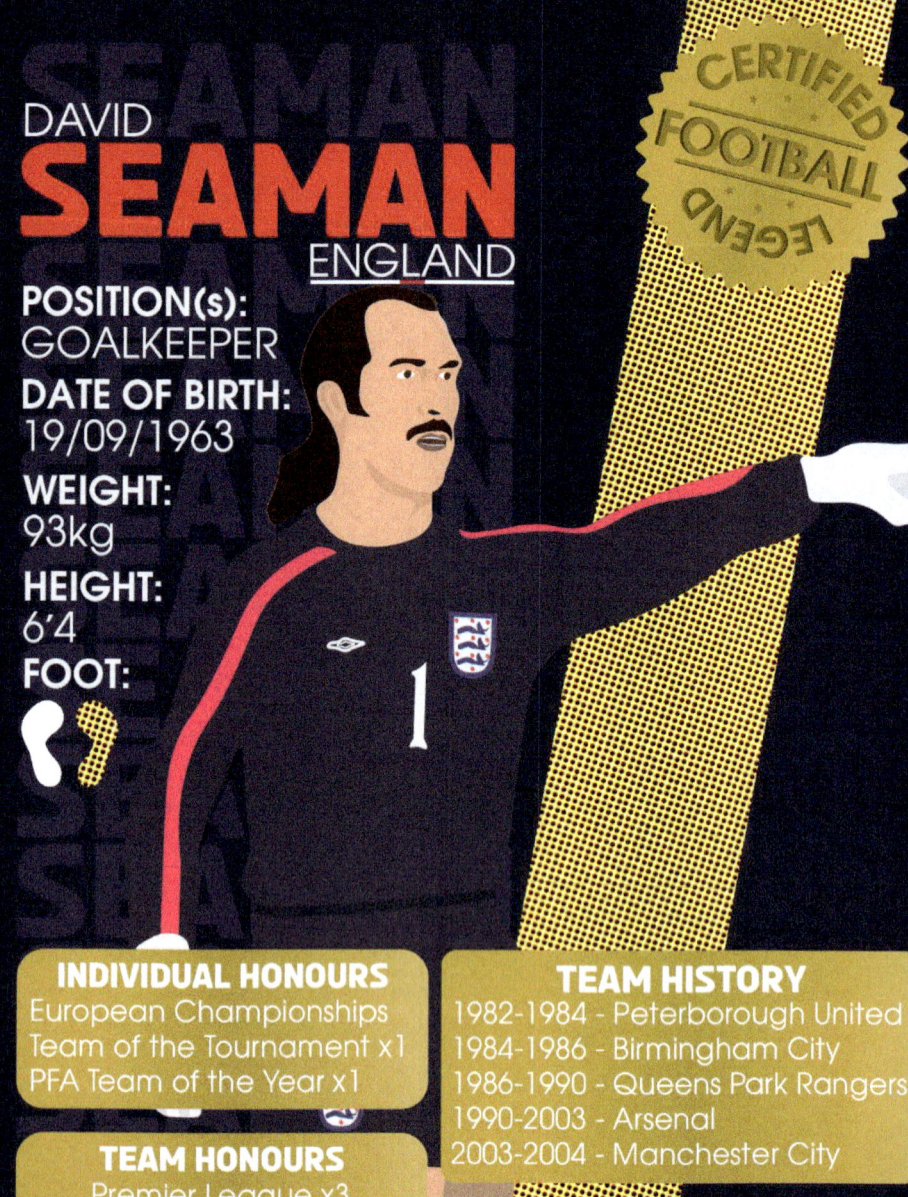

POSITION(s): GOALKEEPER
DATE OF BIRTH: 19/09/1963
WEIGHT: 93kg
HEIGHT: 6'4
FOOT:

CERTIFIED FOOTBALL LEGEND

INDIVIDUAL HONOURS
European Championships Team of the Tournament x1
PFA Team of the Year x1

TEAM HONOURS
Premier League x3
FA Cup x4
League Cup x1

TEAM HISTORY
1982-1984 - Peterborough United
1984-1986 - Birmingham City
1986-1990 - Queens Park Rangers
1990-2003 - Arsenal
2003-2004 - Manchester City

One of England's most successful goalkeepers, David Seaman enjoyed an extremely successful career. He won 75 caps for England, the country's second-most capped goalkeeper, after Peter Shilton, particularly impressing at Euro 96' after being named in the UEFA Team of the Tournament and winning Phillips' Player of the Tournament. Seaman also enjoyed his trophy-laden spell with Arsenal, having joined from QPR in 1990 for a then British record of £1.3million. In just his first season at the Gunners, Seaman conceded just 18 goals in 38 games as Arsenal went on to lift the First Division title.

Seaman would next taste success as Arsenal lifted the FA Cup and League Cup double in 1993, a year before lifting the European Cup Winners' Cup. These cup victories earned Seaman a reputation as a penalty-saving specialist thanks to his heroics during the knockout rounds, which was on display the following year as Arsenal narrowly missed out on retaining their Cup Winners' Cup after losing in the final against Real Zaragosa.

With the introduction of Arsenal legend Arsene Wenger as manager, Seaman would go on to win two domestic doubles in 1998 and in 2002. Arsenal would also reach another major European Final but lost out on penalties to Galatasaray in the 2000 UEFA Cup Final. Seaman ended his Arsenal career in 2003, playing his final game in the FA Cup Final where he would lift the trophy for the fourth time as the Gunners defeated Southampton 1-0.

International Caps	League Games	European Games
75	731	72

MOST CLEAN SHEETS IN INTERNATIONAL FOOTBALL

#	Player	Clean Sheets
1	Iker Casillas	102
2	Gianluigi Buffon	72
3	Hugo Lloris	62
4	David Ospina	61
5	Petr Cech	56
6	Claudio Bravo	55
7	Edwin van der Sar	54
8	Shay Given	52
9	Guillermo Ochoa	52

Accurate as of August 2022

64

> As a goalkeeper, you always expect every team to give you nightmares.
>
> **EDWIN VAN DER SAR**

PETER SHILTON
ENGLAND

CERTIFIED FOOTBALL LEGEND

POSITION(s): GOALKEEPER

DATE OF BIRTH: 18/09/1949

WEIGHT: 81kg

HEIGHT: 6'0

FOOT:

TEAM HISTORY
1966-1974 - Leicester City
1974-1977 - Stoke City
1977-1982 - Nottingham Forest
1982-1987 - Southampton
1987-1992 - Derby County

TEAM HONOURS
First Division x1
League Cup x1
European Cup x2
European Super Cup x1

INDIVIDUAL HONOURS
IOC European Footballer of the Season x1
PFA Players' Player of the Season x1
Nottingham Forest Player of the Season x1
Southampton Player of the Season x2
PFA First Division Team of the Year x10
PFA Team of the Century x1
English Football Hall of Fame x1

England icon Peter Shilton is truly one of the game's greatest ever goalkeepers. With a total of 1390 professional appearances, Shilton is regarded as the most capped player ever in the men's professional game! As well as this, the experienced number one is England's most capped player with 125 international appearances. His stellar career spans over 30 years and with many different clubs, with his most successful period being with Nottingham Forest.

Shilton signed for Forest in their first season back in the First Division under manager Brian Clough, a season that would be one to remember as Forest won the title in their first season back at the top of English football. Shilton's performances were noted as the keeper conceded just 18 goals in 37 games and subsequently won the PFA Players' Player of the Year award for that season. The following season Shilton would lift the Football League Cup as well as Forest's first ever European Cup after a 1-0 victory over Swedish side Malmo. Forest would then retain the European Cup the following year by defeating Kevin Keegan's Hamburg.

Despite his glamorous career, Shilton did not make his World Cup finals debut until the age of 32! However, he would go on to represent England at three World Cups in 1982, 1986 and 1990. He ended up playing in 17 finals matches and even shares the record for most clean sheets in World Cup finals matches with 10 clean sheets, joint with French goalkeeper Fabien Barthez.

International Caps	League Games	European Games
125	1005	25

LEV YASHIN
RUSSIA

POSITION(s):
GOALKEEPER

DATE OF BIRTH:
22/10/1929

WEIGHT:
82kg

HEIGHT:
6'2

FOOT:

CERTIFIED FOOTBALL LEGEND

TEAM HISTORY
1950-1970 - Dynamo Moscow

TEAM HONOURS
Soviet Top League x5
Soviet Cup x3
Euro Championships x1
Olympic Games Gold Medal x1

INDIVIDUAL HONOURS
Ballon d'Or x1
European Goalkeeper of the Year x9
FIFA Goalkeeper of the 20th Century x1
IFFHS World Goalkeeper of the Century X1
USSR Goalkeeper of the Year x3

Nicknamed the 'Black Spider', or the 'Black Panther', Lev Yashin is regarded as one of the best goalkeepers in the history of football. The oldest player to feature in this book, Yashin is credited for revolutionising the goalkeeper position and was known to impose his authority on his defence with his vocality and leadership. Labelled as the first sweeper keeper, Yashin was known for coming off his line to intercept crosses and also ran out to meet onrushing attackers, all during a time when goalkeepers spent the 90 minutes standing in the goal waiting to be called into action.

Yashin appeared in four World Cups from 1958 to 1970 and was chosen as the goalkeeper for the World Team of the 20th Century, the FIFA Dream Team of World Cup history, and was voted the best goalkeeper of the 20th century by the IFFHS. He holds an Olympic Gold medal and a European Championship winners medal with the former Soviet Union, and to this day he is the only goalkeeper to receive the Balon d'Or!

He has also been selected as the Golden Player of Russia by the Russian Football Union as their most outstanding player of the past 50 years! Despite not being as well known as many other goalkeeping legends, Yashin's ability was up there with the greatest of goalkeepers, keeping over 270 professional clean sheets and saving over 150 penalty kicks – more than any other goalkeeper in the professional game.

International Caps	League Games	Clean Sheets
74	326	270

GORDON
BANKS
ENGLAND

POSITION(s):
GOALKEEPER

DATE OF BIRTH:
30/12/1937

WEIGHT:
84kg

HEIGHT:
6'1

FOOT:

CERTIFIED FOOTBALL LEGEND

TEAM HISTORY
1958-1959 - Chesterfield
1959-1967 - Leicester City
1967-1973 - Stoke City

TEAM HONOURS
World Cup x1
League Cup x2

INDIVIDUAL HONOURS
FIFA Goalkeeper of the Year x6
FWA Footballer of the Year x1
FIFA World Cup All-Star Team x1
FIFA 100 x1
English Football Hall of Fame x1
PFA Team of the Century x1

70

Another English goalkeeping legend, Gordon Banks is to this day still widely regarded as one of the greatest goalkeepers of all time. Banks made 679 appearances during a 20-year professional career as well as winning 73 caps for England, including being England's starting goalkeeper for every game during their 1966 World Cup victory.

As well as his heroics in 1966, Banks was ever-present in England's 1970 World Cup run, making one of the game's greatest ever saves to prevent a Pele goal in the group stages of the tournament. However, due to illness, he missed England's quarter-finals match against West Germany as they were knocked out after a 3-2 defeat after extra time.

Banks was recognised for his performances between the sticks as he was named the FWA Footballer of the Year in 1972, the FIFA Goalkeeper of the Year on six occasions and was also the second-best goalkeeper of the 20th century, after Lev Yashin, by the IFFHS. Banks lifted the League Cup on two occasions in addition to the famous 1966 World Cup, but eventually retired in 1973 after a car crash. The Stoke City and England number one suffered a car crash in October 1972 which cost him both the sight in his right eye and, eventually, his professional career.

International Caps	League Games	European Games
73	558	5

MOST PROFESSIONAL APPEARANCES IN GOAL

1	Peter Shilton	1398
2	Paul Bastock	1285
3	Rogerio Ceni	1226
4	Fabio	1210
5	Frantisek Planicka	1187
6	Ray Clemence	1170
7	Gianluigi Buffon	1157
8	Iker Casillas	1125
9	Pat Jennings	1105

Accurate as of August 2022

> As a goalkeeper you need to be good at **organising** the people in front of you and **motivating** them
>
> **PETER SHILTON**

Printed in Great Britain
by Amazon